MW01092385

IMAGES
of America

FARRAGUT NAVAL TRAINING STATION

David G. Farragut
First Admiral of the U.S. Navy

David Glasgow Farragut was born in Tennessee on July 5, 1801. Starting his career as a midshipman at the age of nine, he became a prize commander at age 12.

Admiral David Glasgow Farragut (1801-1870)

Farragut is most remembered for a famous quote given during the battle of Mobile Bay. On August 5, 1864 Rear Admiral Farragut moved his fleet of 14 wooden ships, 4 iron clad monitors, and 10 small gunboats through the channel of Mobile Bay that had been heavily mined. Mines were known as torpedoes at that time. The leading monitor was struck by mines and sank within a few minutes. Other Union ships hesitated, but as Farragut shouted these words, "DAMN THE TORPEDOES! FULL SPEED AHEAD!", the fleet continued and went on to captured and smash the defenses of the Confederate. This victory was Farragut's greatest and shortly after he was promoted to Vice-Admiral. Following the Civil War, by an Act of Congress in 1866, David Glasgow Farragut was made the first admiral of the United States Navy. He died on August 14, 1870 at Portsmouth, New Hampshire.

In 1868 after a life-long career in the Navy, Farragut was asked to run for president. He responded:

> "My entire life has been spent in the Navy. By a steady perseverance and devotion to it, I have been favored with success in my profession, and to risk that reputation by entering a new career at my advanced age, and that career of one of which I have little or no knowledge, is more than any one has a right to expect of me."

The name for this naval station was chosen by President Franklin D. Roosevelt, Commander-in-Chief of all U.S. Armed Forces. No greater tribute could have been paid to the First Admiral. No greater inspiration for the men who served after him.

David Glasgow Farragut is pictured, for whom the Farragut Naval Training Station was named. This tribute to Admiral Farragut is just outside the main visitor's center at Farragut State Park.

ON THE COVER: Taken from the archives of Farragut State Park, this photograph is of a regiment (in this instance 16 boot training companies) in formation in one of the station's massive drill halls.

IMAGES
of America

FARRAGUT NAVAL TRAINING STATION

Gayle E. Alvarez and Dennis Woolford

ARCADIA
PUBLISHING

Published by Arcadia Publishing
Charleston, South Carolina

Printed in the United States of America

Library of Congress Control Number: 2009924698

For all general information contact Arcadia Publishing at:
Telephone 843-853-2070
Fax 843-853-0044
E-mail sales@arcadiapublishing.com
For customer service and orders:
Toll-Free 1-888-313-2665

Visit us on the Internet at www.arcadiapublishing.com

*To the "boots," service school graduates, Ships Service, and support staff
who comprised the Farragut Naval Training Station from 1942 to 1946*

CONTENTS

ACKNOWLEDGMENTS

First and foremost, we would like to thank the people and organizations whose contributions made the completion of the book possible: first to the boards of both the Idaho Military Historical Society and Farragut State Park for their support and cooperation, and second we must recognize the individuals who entrusted their collections to the Idaho Military Historical Society and Farragut State Park. Without these wonderful collections, we could have never produced this publication. A special thank you also goes to Yancy Mailes and Gary Keith, who made us aware of Arcadia's publications and helped us with the initial first steps. A second thank you goes to Gary Keith and Ken Swanson for all of their U.S. Navy terminology assistance to a landlubber. Thank you also to Errin Bair, Farragut park ranger, for all of her assistance and support.

A special thank you also goes to the Idaho State Historical Society, who graciously allowed us to use three images from their archives. Credits to their photographs are abbreviated as ISHS.

All images used in this book are from the collections of the Farragut State Park or the Idaho Military Historical Society unless otherwise noted. The majority are official U.S. Navy photographs.

The following ranks are abbreviated throughout the text: Yeoman, First Class (Y1c); Yeoman, Second Class (Y2c); Yeoman, Third Class (Y3c(R)); Chief Specialist (CSp); Electricians Mate, First Class (EM1c); Hospital Apprentice, Second Class (HA2c); Carpenter's Mate, Second Class (CM2c); Bugler, First Class (Bug1c); Chief Yeoman (CY); Ships Service Man Barber, Third Class (SSM(B)3c); Specialist, Photographic Specialist, Third Class (Sp(P)3c); Seaman, First Class (S1c.); and Seaman, Second Class (S2c.).

On September 15, 1942, the U.S. Naval Training Station Farragut, Idaho, was established. During its tenure, it underwent a number of reorganizations resulting in several name modifications. The term "station" is used throughout the manuscript unless the text is an exact quote.

On June 19, 1944, the ranks of "commandant" and "assistant commandant" were changed to "commander" and "assistant commander." Both titles are used in this manuscript.

Introduction

As the United States entered World War II, the Secretary of War desired to establish a naval training facility away from coastal areas, in his words, "far from coastal bombings," which he believed would occur. The site of Lake Pend Oreille, in scenic northern Idaho, was selected, and the announcement was made on March 28, 1942. Rumor has it that Eleanor Roosevelt selected the site, but this is not true; it was a delegation of three senior naval officers.

The station encompassed 4,050 acres at the southern tip of Lake Pend Oreille. The lake itself has an average elevation of 2,050 feet above sea level. The depth is an average 1,100 feet, but in one location, a sounding line was dropped to 2,800 feet and did not reach the bottom. The lake is so deep that it does not freeze over during winter.

Construction began on April 23, 1942, with an initial projected cost in World War II dollars of $20,000,000 for 20,000 men. It was later raised to $57,000,000 for 30,000 men, but there were also other additions and expansions. In May of that year, Pres. Franklin D. Roosevelt named the station Farragut in honor of Adm. David G. Farragut, a Civil War naval hero. President Roosevelt personally visited the site that September. Although still under construction, Farragut welcomed its first naval recruits, or boots, on September 17, 1942, and by September 30, there were 1,000 recruits in training. On June 7, 1943, the Walter Butler Company, construction contractors for the Farragut Naval Training Station, closed their offices at Farragut. By then, several training companies had already graduated.

Farragut was comprised of six separate camps, each camp accommodating 5,000 recruits and virtually self-sufficient with at least 20 barracks, a mess hall, administration building, parade grounds or drill field, sick bay and dispensary, recreation building, and a drill hall with a swimming pool (a recruit had to be able to swim in order to graduate). The Farragut Naval Training Station's administrative area consisted of a general administration building, service buildings, warehouses, cold storage area, and at that time, the largest laundry in the world. One of the station's camps served as a service school for advanced training for sailors and some of the graduating recruits. It was designed to accommodate 7,500 students.

Roughly two hours after arrival, the new recruit walked out of the receiving unit dressed in navy-issued clothing, sporting a new GI haircut, and carrying his $133 worth of personal belongings, which included a mattress and blanket. He then boarded a bus for the barracks that would be his home for the next 6 to 13 weeks. The day began with reveille at 5:30 a.m. and concluded at 4:30 p.m. The training was intense and by lights out at 10 p.m., the recruits were exhausted and went right to sleep, that is to say, those who were not on guard duty or other detail. There was classroom instruction, rifle ranges, the boat docks with rowing drills, personnel and quarter's inspections, and all that goes with military life. Even so, they still found time for various forms of entertainment and athletic competition. Graduation day brought a promotion to either fireman or seaman second class, which increased the boot's monthly pay from $50 to $54 per month.

As the number of recruits arriving increased, so did everything else. During December 1942, the station post office handled 1,500,000 pieces of first class mail plus 106,000 pieces of parcel post. By April 1943, that number had risen to 2,000,000 pieces and grew to over 3,000,000 by

August, not counting parcel post and magazines. Eventually there were nine Ships Service stores, eight barber shops, a cobbler shop, a haberdashery, a tailor shop, a photography department, nine cafes, and soda fountains.

As the war came to its by now inevitable conclusion, Farragut's role changed, and it transitioned into a neuropsychiatric center and was for a time home to over 800 German POWs. In the spring of 1946, decommissioning began, and in June, the installation was turned over to the Farragut College and Technical Institute, whose focus was on returning veterans. Today a good portion of the site comprises Farragut State Park.

During its heyday, from September 17, 1942, until March 10, 1945, when the last class graduated, Farragut was the second largest U.S. naval training station in the United States and arguably the largest city in Idaho. During the 30 months it was operational, Farragut trained 293,381 recruits from at least 23 states. By August 1945, the number of service school graduates had reached 25,943. This book is Farragut's story.

"These smiling huskies are from Co. 3043, Camp Bennion," reported the June 8, 1944, *Farragut News*. These sailors had just set a new station record for the boat course of 6:01.08. Pictured are, on the left side of the boat from front to back, R. K. Van Houten, Los Angeles, California; A. Amenti, San Francisco, California; J. R. Fraser, Grand Rapids, Minnesota; C. G. Savage, Concrete, Washington; F. Bruning, Missoula, Montana; I. C. Boies, Moorcroft, Wyoming; and F. B. Correa, Los Angeles, California. On the right side from front to back are R. B. Kelly (coxswain), San Francisco, California; A. F. Mackey, Tacoma, Washington; A. W. King, Costa Mesa, California; A. J. Lessard, Duluth, Minnesota; F. T. Bush, San Francisco, California; G. C. Hanson, Los Angeles, California; R. S. Hollingshead, Pasadena, California; C. Bolt, Duluth, Minnesota; and J. Busie, Los Angeles, California. Looking on are Lt. (jg) M. H. Walker, 10th Battalion commander, and E. R. Herlin, CSp(A), Company 3043 commander.

One

IN THE BEGINNING

As the United States entered World War II, the Secretary of War desired to establish a naval training facility "far from coastal bombings," which he believed would occur. On March 19, 1942, three senior naval officers flew over Lake Pend Oreille to inspect the site. On March 28, 1942, the U.S. government issued a press release announcing the decision to locate the station there. This is a preconstruction aerial photograph of the area.

On April 6, 1942, *The Coeur d'Alene Press* announced the news in a banner headline on the front page. Information on the station became a regular part of *The Coeur d'Alene Press*. In 1942, it began running a section each Tuesday called "Farragut Station News," but this was discontinued in 1943 as the war escalated and news about the station was placed in the regular sections of the paper.

The station encompassed 4,050 acres at the southern tip of Lake Pend Oreille. The lake itself has an average elevation of 2,050 feet with an average depth of 1,100 feet. Seven families owned the land the station was built on. Signed options to purchase the land were obtained from the owners, and in federal court on September 21, 1942, the land transfer was finalized.

FARRAGUT NEWS

PAGE TWO

President Visited Farragut On Inspection Tour In September, 1942

This picture, made on September 21, 1942, shows the late President Roosevelt as he moved about the still uncompleted Training Station by automobile. With him on this tour of the Station were, from left to right, Chase A. Clark, then Governor of Idaho, Rear Admiral Ross T. McIntyre, the President's personal physician, and Rear

Admiral I. C. Sowell, then Captain Sowell, first Commandant at Farragut.
F. D. R.'s visit here was a part of his secret nation-wide inspection tour of war activities. It was his second visit to Idaho since becoming President in 1933. He crossed the entire southern part of the state in 1937, stopping

in Boise to visit every school in the city.
Arriving near the Main Gate by train, President Roosevelt went by car through the Station which had been commissioned just a few days before. He expressed great interest in the speed with which the Station was constructed.

World Mourned President Followed

On May 30, 1942, President Roosevelt named the station Farragut in honor of Admiral Farragut, a Civil War hero and first admiral of the U.S. Navy. Four months later, on September 21, 1942, Roosevelt made a secret inspection of war activities and visited Farragut. Shown with the president are, from left to right, Hon. Chase A. Clark, governor of Idaho, Rear Adm. Ross McIntyre, the president's personal physician, and USN Capt. I. C. Sowell, the station's commandant.

On April 10, 1942, the Walter Butler Company of St. Paul, Minnesota, was awarded the construction contract, and they broke ground 13 days later with a six-month deadline for completion. The estimated cost was $20,000,000 for 20,000 men, but was later modified to $57,000,000 for 30,000 men. Prior to construction, 2,000 men were put to work clearing the site. This photograph is of the construction of Camp Waldron's barracks.

Site preparation for the acreage that was to become the Farragut Naval Training Station caused a horrendous dust problem, as the soil was very fine. It so filled the air sometimes that breathing became a real problem. Dust pneumonia reached near-epidemic levels. This photograph is of the construction of barracks 13 and the mess hall in Camp Bennion.

More than 20,000 men worked 10 hour shifts, alternating between six and seven days per week. The Butler Company claimed a peak working force of 25,000 men, and its employees were well paid. Bricklayers earned $1.75 per hour, plumbers $1.55, carpenters $1.40, and laborers $1. Any time worked over 40 hours was time and a half. This photograph is of workers constructing the married officers' quarters.

An attempt was made to save trees from destruction so that they could provide shade, aesthetic beauty, and a degree of camouflage. Access roads and temporary utilities were needed, and hills had to be flattened before work on the station itself could begin. Trees were milled as they were cut, and thus the buildings were constructed with green lumber. The Walter Butler Company recorded that 98,000,000 board feet of lumber went into the camp.

During the construction of the station, 1,800,000 cubic yards of earth were graded, and 46 miles of stone and macadam roads were laid. Railroad tracks totaled 13 miles, sewer lines 34 miles, and water mains 26 miles. As the war escalated, demand for trained naval personnel increased, hence expansion at Farragut. By October 31, 1944, construction costs had reached $64,655,068.80. This photograph is of a barracks and mess hall construction. Note the ever-present dust.

The station had 20 miles of electric transmission lines; the Bonneville Power Administration supplied electric power. All structures had electric lighting, and the station had a complete electric substation. The station also had two diesel generators, one in the powerhouse and a standby generator in the hospital. This photograph is of the central heating plant for the warehouses, with the west water tower in the background.

Urban legend has it that midway through construction, it was discovered that the station's plans had been switched with San Diego's. The reason for the so-called discovery was that flat roofs were being built at Farragut, and San Diego's buildings reportedly had peaked roofs. Although widely perpetuated, the story remains unproven.

There were no sewage treatment plants in the area, so solid waste disposal was a major concern. A treatment facility was constructed, designed to meet the needs of a population of 45,000. It was constructed near the edge of the lake where the material was treated before it was discharged.

The navy decided to hold a grand opening for the first camp to open at the station, even though the station itself was still under construction. The station had been kept off-limits to the general public during construction; there was even a 6-foot-high chain-link fence enclosing it. The publicity also made for a great war bond drive.

15

This preview, or open house, would be the first and only one permitted at the station. Thereafter any visitors would have to be next of kin, and the visits would be restricted to the station's hostess house, which is pictured here. Boots could receive visitors on Sundays between 1:00 p.m. and 4:30 p.m.

The entertainment for the open house was provided by people in the movie industry who came as part of the Hollywood Victory Committee. The event was broadcast coast-to-coast by CBS and emceed by Dick Powell. The number of tickets reached 30,0000, sold at $1.50 each to Butler employees and their families and to the general public. Other celebrities included Chet Huntley and Dale Evans.

Station security was a fact of life. A gatehouse was, according to the *Farragut News*, "as far as visitors get, unless they have a mighty good reason to get inside." Other security included a Jeep patrol car (pictured here in an October 1944 parade) and a patrol boat on the lake, both of which had a two-way radio. The station also had a diaphone system in the event of a fire or other emergency.

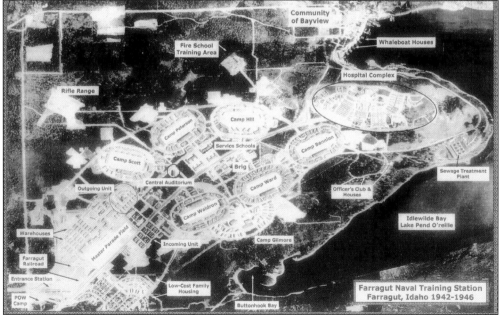

Farragut was comprised of six separate camps, five of which (Bennion, Ward, Waldron, Hill, and Scott) were training camps accommodating 5,000 recruits each. The typical company was 120 recruits, with 20 companies forming a regiment. Each camp was laid out in an oval configuration and was virtually self-sufficient. On August 9, 1942, the first ship's company (full-time personnel) reported for duty, a mere five months after the construction contract was awarded.

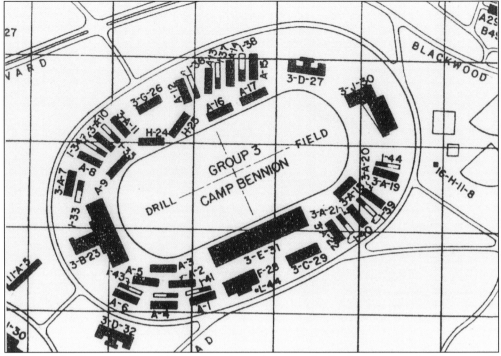

Each camp had between 20 and 22 two-story barracks, a mess hall, administration building, parade grounds or drill field, sick bay and dispensary, recreation building, and a drill hall with a swimming pool. The station's administrative area consisted of a general administration building, service buildings, warehouses, cold storage area, and at that time, the largest laundry in the world.

On September 15, 1942, Area C, sometimes referred to as Area No. 3, was named and commissioned Camp Bennion in honor of Capt. Mervyn S. Bennion, who was killed while serving as commanding officer of the USS *West Virginia* at Pearl Harbor on December 7, 1941. Captain Bennion was posthumously awarded the Medal of Honor. Camp Bennion (Regiment 3) was the first camp to open and begin training recruits at the station.

Following Camp Bennion, Camp Ward opened on October 6, 1942. It was named in honor of James R. Ward, S1c., who was killed in action on board the USS *Oklahoma* on December 7, 1941. Seaman Ward was posthumously awarded the Medal of Honor. This photograph is part of a panorama taken from a 175-foot fire watchtower on Monaghan Boulevard.

The next camp to open was Camp Waldron, which opened on November 8, 1942. It was named for Lt. Comdr. John Charles Waldron, who was killed while commanding the famous Torpedo Squadron 8 at the Battle of Midway. Lieutenant Commander Waldron was posthumously awarded the Distinguished Service Cross.

Camp Hill was opened on December 2, 1942, and was named in honor of Edwin J. Hill, chief boatswain, who was killed in action while serving aboard the USS *Nevada* at Pearl Harbor on December 7, 1941. Chief Boatswain Hill was posthumously awarded the Medal of Honor. Pictured here is a regimental review at Camp Hill on July 22, 1944.

Camp Scott opened on December 19, 1942, and was named in honor of Rear Adm. Norman Scott, who distinguished himself while leading a cruiser division from his flagship aboard the USS *Atlanta* in the Battle of Savo Island on November 13, 1942. Admiral Scott was posthumously awarded the Medal of Honor. This photograph is believed to have been taken from a 175-foot fire watchtower on Monaghan Boulevard.

Camp Peterson opened on March 25, 1943, and was named in honor of Chief Watertender Oscar V. Peterson, who died from wounds received in the Battle of Coral Sea in 1942. He was posthumously awarded the Medal of Honor and was believed to have had a home in Richfield, Idaho. Peterson was a service school with the same layout as the other camps, but with an additional four large classroom buildings, pictured here.

Camp Gilmore opened on June 26, 1944, and was named in honor of Comdr. Howard W. Gilmore, who was posthumously awarded the Medal of Honor for his actions on board the USS *Growler* on February 7, 1943. Gilmore was never used for recruit training, but rather was used for additional training. It had only 21 two-story barracks and had no drill hall or drill field. Part of Gilmore's Recreation Center is pictured here.

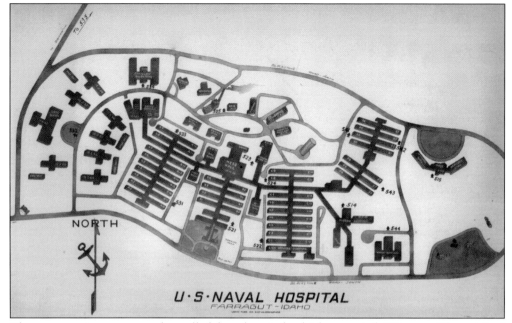

The construction contract also called for a hospital, which occupied 170 acres. The original installation consisted of a complete facility with a capacity of 1,477 beds. The hospital was commissioned and placed in operation on January 17, 1943, by Capt. H. S. Harding (MC), USN. This illustration of the hospital complex is dated June 27, 1944.

Farragut became the second largest naval training station on April 23, 1943, one year after ground was broken. By 1943, bluejackets who had trained at Farragut had seen action against the enemy on many of the war's far-flung battlefronts. Pictured here is an aerial view of camps Scott and Peterson. In the center of the photograph is the brig, the station's prison.

Two

A BOOT'S LIFE

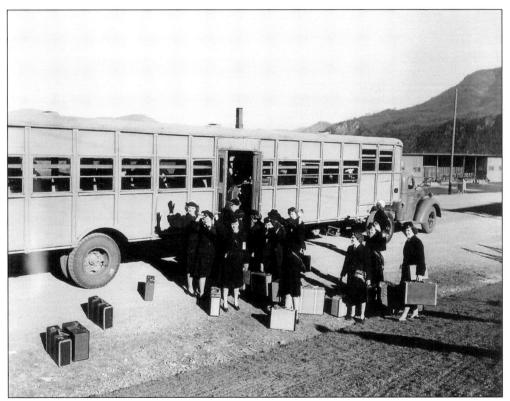

The recruits disembarked, often at night, at nearby Athol, Idaho, and were herded together into cattle cars and trucked to the new station. After a night in a crowded barracks, the future seamen (average age 17) spent their first full day making the transition from civilian to boot. The cattle cars were an equal opportunity mode of transportation; the WAVES who came on board in 1943 also rode in them.

MAIN ENTRANCE GATE AT FARRAGUT is approached by a contingent of happy (?) recruits, about to be transformed from civilians into sailors. This entrance was situated at the corner of the sprawling Naval Training Center, about one-fourth mile southwest of what is now the Farragut State Park Administration Building. From this entrance, Farragut Boulevard stretched about three miles through the recruit training area, and down past the U. S. Naval Hospital to Bayview.

At least 23 states sent recruits to Farragut. They were California, Colorado, Idaho, Illinois, Iowa, Kansas, Massachusetts, Michigan, Minnesota, Missouri, Montana, Nebraska, Nevada, North Dakota, Oklahoma, Oregon, South Dakota, Tennessee, Texas, Utah, Washington, Wisconsin, and Wyoming.

By September 30, 1942, there were 1,000 recruits in training. The new recruits, officially in boot camp and soon to be very conspicuous in their white leggings or "boots," thus became known as "boots." Here a group of boots near Camp Bennion learns how to walk with snowshoes.

Although still under construction, Farragut welcomed its first recruits on Tuesday, September 17, 1942. Jack Eugene Zimmer, pictured here, was the first man to enter Farragut, and he began his training with Camp Bennion's Company 1. Zimmer was part of a group of 61 recruits, 20 of whom were from Portland, Oregon, and 20 who, like himself, were from Denver, Colorado. Zimmer's grades were good, and he received his first choice of secondary schools, Aviation Metalsmith.

The October 1943 station press release accompanying this photograph read, "Having just arrived at this U.S. Naval Training Station, these new recruits are waiting outside the receiving unit. They will be full-fledged bluejackets within an hour and a half, getting a haircut and receiving uniforms, inoculations and a thorough medical and dental examination. Standing in the foreground from left to right are Charles Austin, Opportunity, Wash.; Donald Hughes, Kettle Falls, Wash.; and Donald Wilcox, Spokane, Wash."

Everybody was measured for and then issued clothing and shoes. Roughly two hours after arrival, the new recruit walked out of the receiving unit dressed in navy-issued clothing, sporting a new GI haircut, and carrying his $133 worth of personal belongings, which included a mattress, hammock, and blanket. He then boarded a bus for his barracks, which would be his home for the next six to 13 weeks.

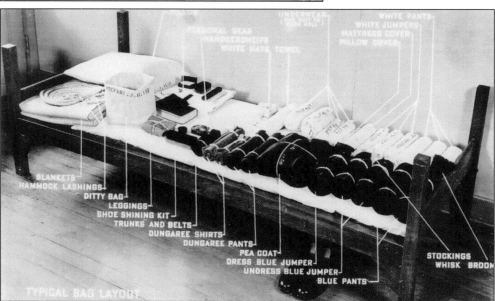

One of a boot's first duties was to stencil his name on everything with the stencil he had just been given. All of his civilian clothes and toiletries, with the exception of razors and toothbrushes, were placed in bags and shipped back to the boot's home. This photograph displays the contents of a boot's sea bag, all the items issued to him upon his arrival and now properly stenciled.

Still wearing civilian clothing, his mind no doubt full of the rumors that have reached him about life in boot camp, these recruits begin the transformation from civilian to boot with their first haircut. Maximum hair length was 3 inches, no tipping was allowed, and rank had no privilege; boot or officer was immaterial, with first come, first served. The barbers, from left to right, are M. C. Garcia, L. J. Perillo, L. M. Alameda, L. S. Burns, J. Nemeth, F. R. Thomas, H. Duvall, R. L. Cline, and S. Orozco.

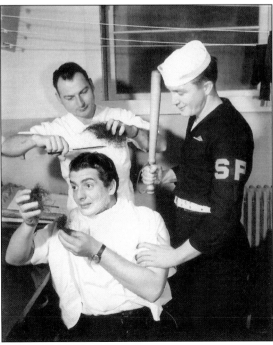

Victor Mature, a prominent Hollywood actor, and Coast Guard chief boatswain, brought his troupe of over 70 entertainers to the station and was promptly told that his 8-inch hair was strictly against regulation. Recruits were often asked if they wanted to keep their sideburns or "locks of glory." If they replied yes, the barber placed the hair in their hands after snipping it off . . . much to the chagrin of the recruit.

Shore Patrolman J. E. Hoage (right), S2c., of Kansas City, Missouri, and barber L. M. Sheller (left), SSM(B)3c, of Rippey, Iowa, pose with a now-shorn Victor Mature (seated). This is actually a doctored photograph; the original caption, which appeared in the *Farragut News*, reads, "It's a sorry looking dejected Mature when the job is finished. But don't worry girls, it's a photographer's gag and Vic is still as handsome as ever. All concerned got a 'boot' out of it."

"SHOTS" were almost a weekly event during "Boot Camp," as new recruits were given inoculations against smallpox, tetanus, yellow fever, and many other health hazards they might encounter during their naval service. Intensive dental treatment also was emphasized during these days, and thousands of teeth were pulled to eliminate the possibility of disabling toothaches during critical months of service. Few of them looked as happy as these young stalwarts from Kansas who posed for this picture.

All incoming recruits were given a complete physical examination. They were then quarantined (not able to leave the station) for three weeks, but even then outbreaks of scarlet fever persisted, resulting in hundreds of cases of rheumatic fever. After the first three weeks were completed, the boots were granted their first liberty. After training began, Friday became inoculation day to allow for recovery from any stiffness or swelling before Monday.

This was the boots' first view of their new home and was also their first brush with navy vocabulary, which they would learn to speak fluently. This is also when they met their company commander, a chief petty officer with the rank of chief specialist. Barracks housed two companies of recruits, one company on the lower deck and the other topside.

FIRST VIEW OF HOME IN THE BARRACKS looked like this. There was no semblance of carpeting, of course, but there were signs to tell you that the "ceiling" now was the "overhead," and the "front" was the "bow." Many other signs introduced the recruit to the Naval terminology of ship life. Each "deck" of the barracks contained about 75 bunks, to accommodate about 150 men. Each recruit was issued his own mattress, and they received heavy canvas hammocks too, which they would need on board ship. Large communal shower and shave rooms adjoined the "heads" at the end of each "deck." Everything was real informal and cosy -- no privacy -- you could always hold hands if you were lonesome!

Each day's activities included a daily flag raising and bugler playing the national anthem. This ceremony was conducted in each recruit area, rain or shine. All traffic stopped during the ceremony, and civilians joined in paying their respect to the flag. This particular photograph was taken on Flag Day in 1944 at the administration field just across from the Central Administration Building.

Here a company on the drill field undergoes their daily physical fitness routine. A letter written home from Camp Ward's Company 452-44 by Donald Allen MacLean stated that the average day began with wake up at 4:45 a.m., bunks were made by 5:15 a.m., chow was at 6, and by 7:30 a.m., they were out on the grinder marching and drilling, which lasted two hours.

The boots' structured training days ended at 4:30 p.m. The training was intense and by lights out, 10:00 p.m., the recruits were exhausted and went right to sleep, that is to say, those who were not on guard duty or other details. There was classroom instruction, rifle ranges, the boat dock, personnel and quarters inspections, and all that goes with military life. Here boots undergo gas mask training.

During their training, boots were indoctrinated into navy life through lectures and training films augmented by intensive classes in seamanship and warfare, along with field-training sessions—all emphasizing teamwork. The long process of becoming regimented, by marching on the grinders (cinder parade grounds) and standing in line for meals and showers, was all part of the U.S. Navy's process of ingraining the boots to follow orders without exception.

At 6 feet, 7 inches tall, Darrell Andrew Crone of Glendale, California, Company 688, Camp Bennion, was too tall for his bunk, and his blue pants only reached his knees. As such, he wore knickers until his uniforms could be tailored. Crone celebrated his 20th birthday on July 11, 1944. This photograph appeared in both the *Farragut News* (the station's newspaper) and *The Coeur d'Alene Press*. The edit marks are still visible.

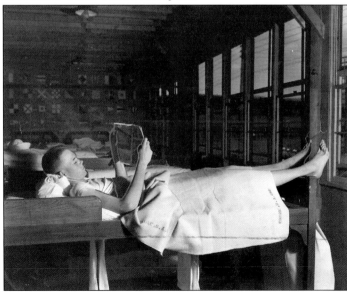

Training adjourned midday Friday, and Friday afternoons became Field Day, which meant a thorough cleaning of the barracks. With so many windows in the buildings, a big part of Field Day was the cleaning of windows with the pumice from bars of Bon Ami.

Interspersed among the barracks were laundry buildings (scrub decks), where the boots would wash their clothes with the lye soap and scrub brushes that were issued to them. The washed clothing was secured to the drying lines by short lengths of corded line (rope ties). In bad weather, the laundry was hung to dry on drying lines inside the laundry buildings.

When weather permitted, clothes would be hung on lines outside, and the boots had to tie the clothing with a square knot. If the drill instructor discovered that a square knot was not used, he would tear the clothing down and stomp on it. Even mattresses were hung on the company clothesline to air out.

Saturday mornings called for personnel inspections and inspections of living quarters. Blankets and bunks had to be spotless, and sea bags containing the recruit's clothing had to be free of any scuff marks and hung meticulously at the end of the bunk. The *Farragut News* noted, "The double-deck bunks, standard sleeping accommodations in the barracks which make no provisions for ex-civilians who walk in their sleep or toss about casually."

This photograph is believed to be Company 18, Camp Bennion, E. C. Dickson, CSp, in October 1943 in their barracks after being named Honor Company of the week, following a rigid inspection of quarters and men. Being designated the outstanding company during an inspection was an honor eagerly sought. Inspections took place every Wednesday and Saturday but could be conducted at any time, day or night.

"Inspection has a personal meaning for every recruit who has done the housework and also brought his personal belongings and appearance up to 4.0 standards," as stated in the *Farragut News*. For personal inspection, a boot's shoes were expected to be sparkling, and his leggings had to be newly washed. Sailors were required to shave daily; no mustaches were allowed. Haircuts were to be obtained at a minimum of every 10 days.

When the words "ready for inspection, sir" are heard, it means that every door and locker is opened or unlocked so that nothing can be stowed away that is not supposed to be seen by the inspecting officer. On one recorded incident, the boot designated to announce the inspecting party forgot his lines and blurted out, "Halt, who goes there?" Laughter suppression efforts were futile; the inspection party moved to the next barracks.

F-10 Marlinspike Instruction

Marlinespike seamanship is the art of handling and working natural fiber, synthetic fiber, and wire rope, often with the use of a marlinspike. It generally covers all types of knot tying, splicing of cordage, sail repair, and fancy rope work. Boots underwent marlinspike instruction in what was called the Rigging Loft. Some of the knots they learned were square knots, clove hitches, bowlines, half hitches, Becket bends, and figure six knots.

This September 1943 station press release read, "Practical instruction in marlinespike seamanship is given recruits at this U.S. Naval Training Station. Recruits from Company 591, Camp Hill, are shown making a cargo net. Cargo nets are used on the station's obstacle courses." From left to right are Harold Murray, Alfred Burckle, Robert Tegeler, Lee Pinckard, Roland Rohn, and John Macaulay.

Semaphore is the navy's way of communicating between ships and stations. By the time recruits headed to sea, all knew the semaphore from A to Z. The semaphore alphabet was even painted on the interior walls of the barracks.

"These brothers, in training together in Company 642, Camp Ward, are spelling out a word all sailors should know. From the top: Gerald, 18, Marven, 19, Lonnie, 20, and Everett Dale Weed, of Orient, Iowa. Their father, age 44, is in the Navy, too, but he is training at Great Lakes. They also have an older brother in the army . . . The word they are spelling is 'Navy,'" according to information from an undated station press release.

After the Saturday inspection, all the bluejackets assembled for a grand pass in review on a 14-acre drill field. Each camp had a drill field, and the station also had a main drill field. The main field was complete with bleachers and had a seating capacity of 6,000. This photograph is titled "Parade Day and View of Grandstand" and gives a perspective of the actual size of the field.

From noon on Saturday until Monday morning reveille, the boots had time to relax. Each camp had a recreation center, which provided entertainment for the off-duty boot, and a recreation director to assist with any recreation needs. Here boots Scott, St. John, Hank, and Moffat shoot a game of pool. Recreation centers had an eight-lane bowling alley in the basement, five tennis tables, two shuffleboards, and a piano.

On Sundays, the boots could attend church services. The station had two chapels, each with a seating capacity of 600. The chapels, the Houston and the Lexington, were used primarily by the officers. Church services for the enlisted were held in the drill halls.

The Houston Chapel was named in honor of the USS *Houston*, which was sunk in Sunda Straits after the Battle of Java Sea on February 28, 1942. Robert E. Whaley, EM1c, pictured here in front of the Houston Chapel, was a crew member on the *Houston*, but he was wounded and put ashore about three weeks before the ship was lost.

The Houston Chapel was dedicated on February 28, 1943, a year to the date of the ship's loss. The commander of the USS *Houston*, Capt. Albert H. Rooks, was posthumously awarded the Medal of Honor. The Houston Chapel also had a choir, and at least one marriage was performed within its walls. This photograph is of part of the interior of the Houston Chapel.

The Lexington Chapel, named in honor of the USS *Lexington*, was dedicated on March 7, 1943. The *Lexington* participated in the May 1942 Battle of the Coral Sea, and as such, she became the target of Japanese carrier planes. After being racked by gasoline explosions and out of control fires, she was abandoned by her crew and scuttled. The *Lexington* became the first U.S. aircraft carrier to be lost in World War II.

The *Service Schools Student Handbook* stated, "IDENTIFICATION CARDS & TAGS All hands, except officers and chief petty officers, must wear their identification cards and <u>two</u> tags around their necks at all times... Do not take them off at any time except when in the showers . . . The loss or alteration of these cards or tags is a serious matter and strong disciplinary action will be taken . . . for your own protection, report any loss of identification cards or tags AT ONCE."

It was not just the military personnel who needed identification cards or badges; civilians needed them, too. On the left is the identification button worn by Alice Hansen, an employee at the station. On the right is a civilian identification card issued to Virginia Phipps.

It was not until 1944 that passenger service between Spokane, Washington, and the station was established on a regular daily schedule. The Spokane International Railroad, on tracks owned by the Northern Pacific, provided the service. The service ran both ways, and each trip took an hour and a half. Eventually three trains made the run. Here sailors board a troop train leaving the station in June 1944 for their next duty station.

Pictured here is the Liberty Train, which ran between Farragut and Spokane. Round-trip fare was $1.10, one cent more than a one-way fare. The sign on the back reads, "Blue Jacket Special, Farragut, Ida."

F-2 Swimming Instruction

Swimming was not just a leisure activity. It was estimated that 30 percent of the recruits could not swim when they enlisted in the navy. The goal was to teach the nonswimmers to swim within the three weeks of the quarantine period. In order to graduate, a boot had to learn how.

Along with swimming, boots also learned lifesaving, how to abandon ship, and how to swim in burning oil. In order to prove he could swim, a boot had to meet a 75-yard standard in the final test. Here Jack Weeden, HA2c, from Alameda, California, masters the task.

The sailor on the right is Stanley W. Legowik, S2c., from Great Falls, Montana, of the station's audio-visual education office, putting the finishing touches on his painting. Paintings such as these were part of the training process and adorned the walls of the station's swimming pools. Legowik's painting depicts one method of abandoning ship. The artist on the left is believed to be Phillip L. Stone.

On the right, James Beird, S2c., of Chicago works on his mural depicting survivors of an abandon ship situation reaching a beach. The mural on the left was painted behind the serving line in one of the mess halls. Sule V. Oja of Ishpeming, Michigan, on the left, and Howard Petrey of Superior, Wisconsin, on the right, remind boots not to waste food.

Murals were not limited to training areas. This photograph is believed to be Phillip L. Stone, United States Navy Reserve (USNR), painting one of two murals that graced the Officers Club. The second painting was very similar to this one and had a winter scene; each painting adorned a side of the fireplace. The winter scene painting is now in the possession of Farragut State Park.

Although not apparent to the novice, these are actually dummy rifles. Every recruit at the station spent countless hours drilling with one of these U.S. Navy Mark 1 dummy rifles. Boots graduated from the dummy rifle to a .22 caliber and eventually to the shoulder-jolting 30.06 rifle.

The barracks buildings and camps were kept safe by recruits on guard duty carrying a U.S. Navy Mark 1 dummy rifle. Here a solitary boot guards the Central Administration Building. A letter written home from the station in 1944 stated that guard duty averaged every other night and lasted between two and four hours.

Physical fitness was promoted by running obstacle courses, long marches with the company, close order drills with dummy rifles, swimming, and other athletic activities in the drill hall. This photograph was published in the June 29, 1944, edition of the *Farragut News* and was used to illustrate that the upcoming Fourth of July holiday was "just another working day" at the station.

Marching was a fact of life at Farragut, and to the boots, the drill instructors seemed merciless. Returning veterans recall the endless miles and hours spent marching everywhere they went. Keeping the boots in shoes was a horrendous nightmare. Drill fields, or grinders as they were called, literally tore shoe soles to pieces. Summer temperatures of 115 degrees did not help matters any. A new pair of shoes lasted about eight days.

The training camps had rifle ranges with firing positions for 40; the station itself had several outdoor ranges shared by all camps. The ranges had few windows; the walls and backs of the targets were constructed of steel sheeting. The outdoor ranges were a 200-yard 100-target range, a 500-yard 10-target range, a 25-yard 12-target pistol range, a 50-yard 12-target pistol range, and a 20-millimeter range on Blackwell Point.

RIFLE RANGE was carved out of a scenic corner of the Farragut grounds, and the hike through the pines down to this area was a welcome change of pace for many recruits. One hundred men could fire at a time, and many remembered the jolting recoil of the 30.06 rifles as a rather unpleasant experience until they learned to hold the gun-stock tightly against the shoulder. About 12,000 rounds of ammunition were fired daily on this range during the peak of training.

Boots sharpened their rifle skills on the Camp Scott Rifle Range by firing rounds from prone and sitting positions at 10-inch bull's-eye targets 200 yards away. The rifle range was one of the country's largest, and the lead and brass were salvaged and used to remake ammunition. The range was so large that a public address system was used to give the commands.

Boots helped their classmates hone their skills by scoring their targets. One source stated that if the boot missed his target completely, a red flag was raised over the target. This was referred to as "Maggie's Drawers" and meant that the boot was off to the kitchen to peel potatoes.

RIFLE RANGE "BUTTS" were an interesting of training during the last weeks of "Boot Camp." These budding men-o'-war have reve..ted the large targets into the concrete pits to repaint the 10-inch bulls-eyes and place indicators over the bullet holes. The targets are then pushed back up above ground level so men on the firing line 200-yards away can spot their shots and adjust their aim accordingly.

Each of the station's six camps had one of these immense drill halls. They were located midway between the mess hall and the recreation center. This photograph is titled "Regimental Drill Hall" and is believed to be the drill hall at Camp Bennion.

The navy allowed few photographs of drill hall interiors, as their construction was somewhat classified. They had no internal supports; all the supports were along the edges. The drill halls contained six basketball courts, a 75-foot-by-75-foot swimming pool, a boxing and wrestling ring, lecture rooms, an altar for religious services, a movie screen with seating to accommodate 2,000, and they still had room for the schools to hold formations.

The first triplets to enter the station, from left to right, Robert, Roy, and Ray Derickson of St. Paul, Minnesota, share a malted milk. The brothers celebrated their 18th birthday on August 19, 1944. Aside from the fact that Roy is 6 inches taller than his brothers, they act, dress, and look alike. This photograph appeared in both the *Farragut News* and *The Coeur d'Alene Press*, and the edit marks are still visible.

Wesley Ross, S2c., of Spokane, Washington, weighs in at 240 pounds and stands 6 feet 6 inches tall. Dominic DeRose, CM2c, of Chicago, Illinois, is 160 pounds and 5 feet and a half-inch tall. This photograph appeared in the May 17, 1945, *Farragut News* and included a lengthy article about a boxing match turned grudge match. The truth of the matter, as is evidenced by the photograph, is they are actually good friends.

The boot's training included lifeboat training. Down at the dock, they raised and lowered lifeboats or whaleboats as if they were on a ship. The dock also contained 90 whaleboats, sailboats, and large 50-foot motor launches that were the same as those that would take sailors ashore from their ships at anchor.

The whaleboats were made of steel, could hold up to 16 persons, were 28 feet in length, and had 19-foot oak oars. The boots spent hours in all weather conditions in these boats, training to row in unison and learning a valuable lesson in teamwork. Each company had a rowing team, and competitions and championships were held each training session. Pictured here is Camp Hill's Company 60-43 team.

There was a marked course of 1,219 yards, and competition to break the course record was fierce. Here Camp Bennion's 823-44 claims bragging rights with a time of 5:45. Team members were, from left to right, (first row) Henry F. Cook, unidentified, James Workman, Marten Tate, Russel L. Gibson, and Ray Maki; (second row) Ted Eide, James Beal, unidentified, Robert A. Wickman, Vernon Bell, Phillip L. Anderson, Art Brossoit, and Chief M. E. North.

Camp Bennion had an excellent record when it came to camp competitions. There are a number of Camp Bennion photographs depicting winning teams from various competitions. This is Class 750-43 displaying proof of their superior seamanship at a number of qualifying events. Their commander was A. M. Faison, and the class graduated on October 21, 1943.

Members of Camp Bennion's Company 68, under Chief Specialist W. L. Colombo, climb an obstacle course's cargo net. The February 27, 1943, *Farragut News* stated, "Spring sunshine makes the task of learning to abandon ship by the use of a cargo net a pleasant task." The boots rapidly ascend and descend the net, and this exercise was part of the station's physical fitness program, which "is doing an excellent job of hardening its men."

This November 1943 station press release read, "This recruit knows the value of physical conditioning as it came in handy while he was in the Canadian Army and engaged in raids upon German-occupied Europe. Shown going over a wall on the obstacle course at this U.S. Naval Training Station is Richard E. Young, 22, from Omaha, Nebraska. He hopes to join his brother, Robert, also in the Naval service."

Here boots at Camp Ward practice valuable training in abandon ship drills and learning how to climb up and down cargo nets. It is also a practical learning experience in the importance of marlinspike seamanship. Note the abandon ship mural mentioned earlier on the side of the wall. A photograph taken seconds prior to this one appeared in the April 6, 1944, *Farragut News.*

No skill taught at the station was more important than the control of shipboard fires. One of the training facilities was the firefighting school, which went into operation on July 10, 1944. It was a two-day course of instruction and could train 1,200 recruits a week. In specially designed concrete buildings and huge tanks built to simulate ship conditions, recruits learned to fight shipboard fires fed by broken fuel lines during battle.

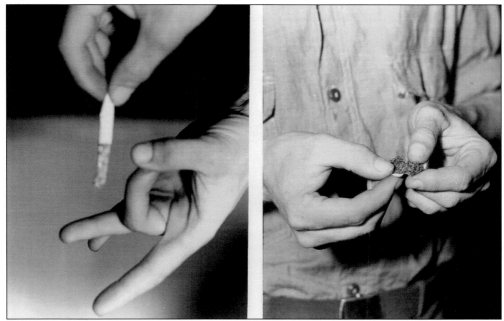

Forest fires were a real and ongoing concern for the station and could easily be ignited by a carelessly tossed cigarette. These photographs were published in the August 14, 1943, *Farragut News* along with detailed instructions on how to properly extinguish a cigarette. It entailed three steps: 1. Flick lighted end off, 2. Break open the cigarette to show it's extinguished, and 3. Roll paper into a ball to show it's out.

This January 1944 station press release read, "This auxiliary fire equipment at Camp Bennion, a pressure booster, can be hauled and operated by recruits—just in the event no trucks are available. It is manned by members of Company 950. In practice runs, the company made the longest run in the camp in five and one-half minutes, and that was from the time the men were given the alarm in their barracks. Company commander (left) is U.L. Odson, chief specialist and former Minnesota football star, while J.D. Cassidy, regimental chief petty officer, looks on at the rear." It was not just shipboard fires or fires at the station that boots were trained to fight. On a number of occasions, boots helped fight forest fires near the station.

Smoking was heavily controlled and only allowed in certain places and at certain times. The Smoke Harbor or Smoking Pit was open only when pails were in the pit, after breakfast until 7:45 a.m., from 11:20 a.m. to 12:50 p.m., and from 4:20 to 8:30 p.m. Posted rules stated there was no smoking before breakfast, when the red or church flags were up, during the captain's inspection, or when there was no guard on duty.

Work details were a fact of life at the station. This station press release read, "It's got to look good and these Bluejackets from a company in Camp Ward are doing their bit in the 'Spring' clean-up of the Farragut Naval Training Center."

This station press release read, "These Spokane, Wash. Recruits at Farragut Naval Training Center are returning to their barracks after working on a 'cleanup' detail, which is part of the regular work schedule for men in 'boot' camp. Left to right, they are: Frank Perno, age 23, Don Peirce, age 22, Wesley Anderson, age 21, and Floyd Katsell, age 23."

In June 1945, the West Coast Overflow was established, which billeted and processed for transfer roughly 500 men per month. The men pictured here just completed a rigorous physical exam and are waiting transport to Camp Gilmore. Many were from the Commander Western Sea Frontier; most were without complete gear or records, or awaiting transfer. They were primarily sent to Farragut for dental work and were billeted and medically cleared.

"What do we do next . . . Seems to be the question ex-Great Lakes Recruits are asking Edward Galiano, CSF, of Hammond, Indiana. These men are part of more than 2,000 men assigned to West Coast Overflow Unit at Camp Waldron. The Chief instructs the men in stowage of gear, their duties and what to expect while at Farragut." This photograph and caption were published in the July 12, 1945, *Farragut News*.

"This Bluejacket wouldn't be able to do any good on the high seas with these snow shoes, but they are a big help at this U.S. Naval Training Station in northern Idaho, where there has been plenty of snow this winter." During its first year of operation, the station received 11 feet of snow and temperatures reached 30 degrees below zero. Bill Trenholm of Astoria, Oregon, seems to be taking it all in stride.

58

Boots were tasked to clear the walkways, but as Farragut had no snow removal equipment at first, they became human snowplows, clearing the snow by marching between the barracks and mess hall. A boot would march in front for about 15 minutes, then go to the rear, and the next boot would step forward. After the first winter, the peacoat was lengthened, providing better protection from frostbite and hypothermia.

Pictured is Hayes Carlen Jr., singing "I Love Life." Prior to enlisting in the navy, Carlen was a member of Sonja Henie's Hollywood show. He reportedly skated in nearly every state in the United States.

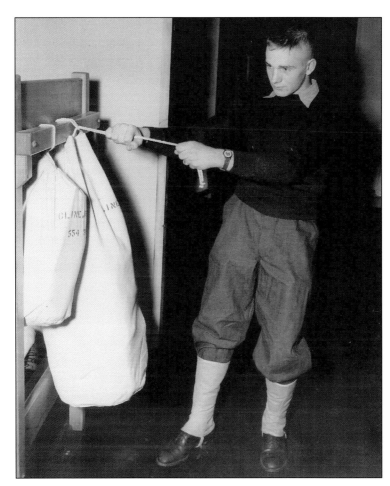

Randall W. Cline, 18, of Kuna, Idaho, a member of Company 965 at Camp Waldron, demonstrates the proper technique of tying one's sea bag to the bunk. As it turned out, Cline was the last recruit to pass through the station, closing the door as it were on December 5, 1944. Between his entrance and that of Zimmer's just 30 months prior, a total of 293,381 recruits passed through the station.

On graduation day, boots took off their "boots" for the last time and then marched over to have their class photograph taken. Each graduating recruit company was photographed, and individual pictures were made available to those who desired them. This is the graduation photograph of the station's first graduating class, Company 1, 11th Battalion, 3rd Regiment. G. C. Owens was the company commander. Their graduation date was November 26, 1942.

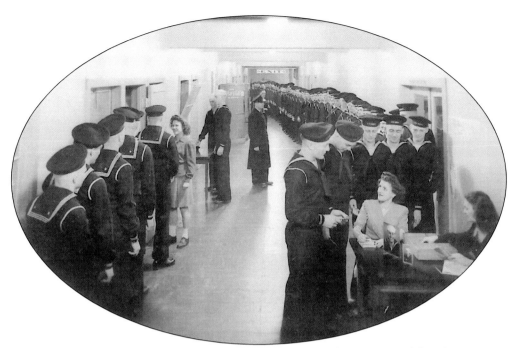

Ross Hall, a well-known photographer from Sandpoint, was the manager of the Ships Service Studio. It was reported that he could take the photograph of a company of 120 men in 30 minutes, taking 3-inch-by-5-inch poses of each man. One thousand large company pictures and over 5,000 individual pictures were processed a day by 30 civilians and 15 naval personnel. Here the new graduates are placing their photograph orders.

In order to take and process that many photographs, Ross Hall utilized three cameras operated by local girls he had hired to help him. During the month of March 1944, there were 20,891 boots who graduated, the highest number recorded for the station. The class photographs also came with a roster listing the names of those in the picture.

"The Outgoing Unit is Grand Central for the men of Farragut off to Service Schools or duty on the Seven Seas." When graduation day finally arrived, boots were automatically promoted from apprentice seaman to either fireman second class or seaman second class. With this promotion, their pay was raised from $50 to $54 per month. On this day, the company roster was posted, indicating what their next assignment would be.

R.M. SCHOOL - CLASS 24-44 - SEC. 108-109-110 - U.S. NAVAL TRAINING CENTER - FARRAGUT, IDAHO - OCT. 6, 1944

For some, the next assignment was a service school in another state or a receiving unit on the coast for assignment to a ship. For others, it was a Farragut service school, which meant more barracks living and stowing belongings in a sea bag. Even so, they no longer had to wear "boots," and had liberty every other weekend. Pictured here is a Farragut service school class of radiomen.

Not all of Farragut's boots graduated. This young fellow managed to slip through the system at the tender age of 12. When he was found out he was sent home. There were a number of recorded instances of underage boots at the station, but this young lad was the youngest recorded.

At least three of Farragut's boots went on to earn a place in history. Robert E. Bush graduated with Camp Hill's Company 28-44, Regiment 4, Battalion 15, on February 15, 1944. He then continued at Farragut, graduating from the Hospital Corps School on or about April 28, 1944. He went on to become a navy medical corpsman, and during the Battle of Okinawa at the age of 18, he became the youngest sailor to receive the Medal of Honor during World War II.

Fredrick F. Lester graduated on December 21, 1943, with Camp Ward's Company 954-43, Regiment 2, Battalion 7. He is pictured here in the third row, the sixth person from left to right. He served as a navy medical corpsman during the Battle of Okinawa, where he earned the Medal of Honor on June 8, 1945. Regrettably, it was a posthumous award.

John H. Bradley trained at Farragut, although his graduation date is unknown. On February 21, 1945, while serving as a hospital corpsman with a marine rifle platoon, he earned the Navy Cross for heroism. He was also one of the flag raisers at Iwo Jima and is in the famous photograph of the second flag raising. His story was made into the book *Flags of our Fathers* as well as a motion picture by the same title. (Courtesy of James Bradley.)

Three

SERVICE SCHOOLS

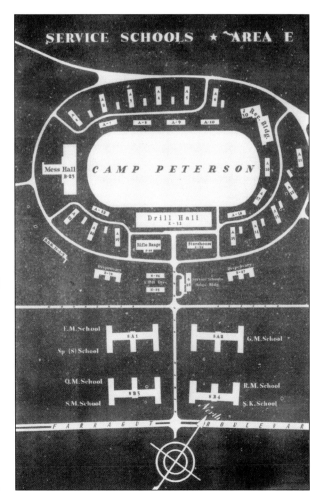

The station was not only a training center for boots, but it also had service schools for cooks and bakers, radiomen, quartermasters, signalmen, storekeepers, gunner's mates, electrical personnel, shore patrol, instructors, and classification interviewers. The service schools were initially located at Camp Peterson but later moved to Camp Gilmore. The map pictured here was published in the *Service Schools Student Handbook*. At any one time, there were 264 companies training there.

The station also had a corpsman school, but it was an adjunct of the hospital and was not located at Camp Peterson. Chief pharmacists mates with many years of service in the U.S. Navy Hospital Corps were among the instructors at the corpsman school. Posing with their commander are, from left to right, (first row) R. L. Acker, R. H. Blackburn, C. W. Virtue (commander and author of the song "Up Farragut"), C. D. Jackson, and L. F. Holiman; (second row) M. L. Playfair, C. R. Cassell, A. R. Thomas, and H. O. Wylie.

Navy schools were varied but the courses were intensive. Here a future gunner's mate learns his trade. By April 15, 1945, the 10 service schools had graduated a combined total of 25,943 students.

Originally believed to be a photograph of a signal corps class, this is actually the audio-visual department, which was located at Camp Waldron. Standing on the left is Lt. Bertram L. Gustafson, USNR, officer in charge of the department. Seated at his right is Stan Gelling, Sp(P)3c, who drew most of the cartoons for the *Farragut News* in his spare time.

On July 1, 1944, the service schools moved from Camp Peterson to Camp Gilmore, which opened on June 26, 1944. Sailors pictured here move their gear from Peterson to Gilmore; note the cleaning gear along with the bedrolls.

"Students of the Service School get 16 weeks packed with rigorous schooling but because men selected for the schools rate high in mentality, they absorb the vast amount of instruction readily." The student sailors pictured here are entering building 8-B-3 in Camp Peterson, which housed the quartermaster and signalmen schools. This photograph and caption were published in the station's souvenir booklet, which was printed just prior to the station's decommissioning.

Service school graduates also had a class photograph taken. The first service school graduates, a class of radiomen, graduated on May 1, 1943. Ironically the camp was still under construction when the last of the six training camps was named on March 25, 1943. Less than three months later, on June 7, 1943, the Walter Butler Company, construction contractors for the station, closed their offices at Farragut.

Four

LIBERTY AND ENTERTAINMENT

Camp shows, band concerts, and speeches from the skipper were presented in what were probably the largest auditoriums the boots had ever seen. The main auditorium, pictured here, had a grand opening that was announced in the January 2, 1943, *Farragut News*. It had two 35-milimeter motion picture projectors, a stage "complete with all accessories," band equipment, and seating capacity for 3,000.

Along with competitive sports and recreation center activities, sailors were also able to take in stage shows. Weekly shows were available at the auditorium, and the publicity for them promised "legitimate drama to vaudeville." Stage talent shows became so popular at the station that two-night runs became accepted. The April 17, 1943, *Farragut News* announced, "Crowds thronging into the auditorium each week have assumed Premiere proportions."

This show was called *Hill-Arities* and was "entirely recruit talent," according to a *Farragut News* article. A May 1943 station press release read, "A colorful and impressive 'V for Victory' was formed by a chorus of bluejackets as a grand finale for the recent stage show presented by Camp Hill recruits in the Central Auditorium of this second largest U.S. Naval Training Station. The show was directed by Lieutenant T. J. Kig, USNF, Regimental Commander at Camp Hill."

Many celebrities and entertainers visited the station to entertain the sailors. Pictured here are bandleader Kay Kyser and his wife, Georgia Carrol. These programs were provided under the supervision of the welfare department then headed by Lt. Comdr. Stanley G. Witter, USNR, a longtime head of the Spokane Parks Department in civilian life.

Charles Pedrino of Company 116, Camp Waldron, a jockey prior to arrival at the station, rode under the name "Rusty Ryan." As a gag, the Central Auditorium staff outfitted him as pictured here. The jockey clothing came from the prop room and a carpenter "dreamed up the horse," according to the March 9, 1944, *Farragut News*, where this picture was published.

Pictured is the station's bus depot, located near the hospital, which provided busses for what was called Liberty Leave Transportation. Sailors were bused to either the USO building in Coeur d' Alene (located on the waterfront where the Coeur d'Alene Resort now sits) or to a USO facility in Sandpoint. Only sailors in good standing with grades above a 2.5 grade point average were permitted liberty. Here station personnel board a bus to a football game in Moscow, Idaho.

The September 28, 1944, *Farragut News* reported that weekly goodwill excursions would begin in order to create a closer bond of friendship between Canada and the United States. These were sponsored by the Sandpoint USO, and the trips were made every Sunday, weather permitting. Pictured here are a group of sailors and their invited guests taking in the beauty of the Kaniksu National Forrest on their way to the border.

Sailors also made a stop at the Bonners Ferry Ranger Station to see firsthand how the scattered forest lookouts keep in touch with their headquarters. Lee White, associate forester, explains the communications system as Edith Foss of Sandpoint works the switchboard.

At the border, sailors are met by the Canadian immigration staff at the customs house (pictured here). Credentials are inspected there before they are permitted entry into Canada. For many of the sailors, this is the first time they have set foot on Canadian soil. This particular excursion took place in October 1944 and was sponsored by the Elks Club.

"Ship models made by recruits from Camp Waldron . . . will be put on display at the Fox Theater in Spokane in connection with the musical revue, 'Here Comes Farragut,' for Navy Relief on September 16th. Making final preparations on an aircraft carrier are, left to right, Stanley W. Legowik and Ralph Gray. Both are seamen second class in the Audio-Visual Education department," according to a September 1943, station press release. Also pictured are a camouflaged destroyer tender and a submarine.

Ships Service also had their events. Chief's dances and officer's Halloween dances were held, as were noon dances, which were often provided for Ships Service personnel in the Recreation Building. Civilian employees as well as WAVES participated in these pleasant interludes. Here Max Gearheart, Bug1c, and Laura Ellen Raymond, S1c., enjoy a brief respite during a Tuesday night WAVE dance.

F-13 Ship's Service Store

Recreation centers provided a place to relax and included a soda fountain, merchandise area, two barber shops with eight chairs each, a spacious library upstairs, and on the main floor was a game room with pool tables and table tennis. Pictured here is the cafeteria section of a Ships Service store located in one of the recreation centers.

Boots also used the recreation centers to hold songfests, write letters home, and read magazines or books. Reading material in the recreation center included the station newspaper, *Farragut News*, as well as *Newsweek* and *Stardom*. Note the training murals on the wall directly above the relaxing sailors. Murals such as this adorned many of the walls at the station. The station's audio-visual education department painted most of them.

Welfare and recreation included recreational expeditions, which commenced on May 30, 1943. Most took place near the station; the starting point was the station's hospital sign on Farragut Boulevard at 10 a.m. They could also be arranged on Sundays through the duty officer. These were limited to four hours and had to be made up of at least three persons. The May 1943 *Farragut News* also reported that they were "excellent physical conditioners."

The expeditions included "timberline chow" box lunches. In order to get the lunches, sailors had to sign up in advance with the librarian in their camp's recreation center. A summary of the facilities of the station dated May 1, 1945, stated, "The land within and outside the Center affords many hiking trails, including mountain climbing." The white sailor hat replaced "flattops" for liberties at the station on May 1, 1944.

"Ski party poses along highway by the sign which directs them a few hundred feet up the slope toward the cozy and rustic ski lodge which is maintained by the State of Idaho and open to the public. Lunches, soft drinks, and beer are available at the lodge," according to the *Farragut News*. From left to right are Bob Howard, Y1c; June Gorman; Bob Henry, Y2c; Billie Hill; Mrs. Albert Novack; and Albert Novack, CY.

"Competitive sports have an important role in the physical fitness program at Farragut Naval Training Center. These Utah recruits are shown in a softball game at one of the Farragut training camps. At bat is Jay Bankhead 18, Wellsville, and the catcher of the opposing team is LaMar George, 18, Logan, Utah. Bankhead's teammates, awaiting bat, are Courtney Brown, 21, Hyrum, and left, George Merrill, 21, Trenton," according to an undated station press release.

Camp Scott's softball team won the Station Baseball Championship in October 1943. Each camp had a team; even the fire department had one. The men pictured here were part of Company 662. From left to right are (first row) Jack Slewinski, Elmer Soehl, Vernon Hansian, John Harrington, Earl Gartin, Al Fabbin, and Elmo Blake; (second row) Howard Manson, William Davis, Bill Zavales, H. H. Ferris (CSP), Dick West, Boyd Glover, Cliff Dover, and John Grill (manager).

Farragut had a varied sports program. Along with softball, there were boxing matches, football games, bowling teams, basketball championships, and even rowing competitions. Individuals could also engage in fishing or swimming, or even take a jujitsu class. The *Farragut News* began featuring the ongoing sporting activities in a sports section not long after it began publication. Here two camps engage in a football skirmish; each camp had a team.

Each camp also had a band. The January 9, 1943, *Farragut News* stated bands were to "keep spirits high by keeping the instruments hot." Band members were highly regarded, as "high praise was heaped on the heads of men furnishing their services." Bands were to play for drilling companies on the various grinders and provide military airs for every other need in the regiments.

In January 1944, the station band department was formed and comprised all station bands and orchestras. Two bands were to play every night, and on Saturday, each band was to play in some part of the station. Even the hospital had a band; pictured here is the Hospital Personnel Musical Parade in February 1945.

A village picnic, a family day of sorts, was held in July 1945. It included many family activities such as sack races, wheelbarrow races, tugs of war, and pie-eating contests. A 23-piece hospital band was also on hand to enliven the festivities. Here the winner of a pie-eating contest is being announced. Notice the identification badge the gentleman in the center is wearing.

Sailors and Ships Service personnel also had furry companions, and many of the camps had mascots. Camp Scott had Maggie. Camp Waldron had Skippy, "a shiny, black cocker spaniel," according to the *Farragut News*, and the sailors built an elaborate doghouse for their friend with logs and plywood floors, walls, and ceilings. At least one graduating company included their mascot in their company photograph: Company 58-43, which graduated on March 8, 1943.

Flip, a cocker spaniel, poses with her day-old pups. Flip came from the Aleutians and lived in Camp Ward with her proud owner, R. B. Sands, CGM, of the camp's ordinance department. The *Farragut News* also had stories about a litter of dachshunds, a pet squirrel, and even a pet skunk.

Bambi, a mule deer, made its home near the brig. She was first mentioned in the *Farragut News* in the September 18, 1943, edition, and soon became somewhat of a regular feature. She always arrived on scene three times a day, at mealtime. There are also reports of several other deer seeking refuge and companionship at the station. A fawn named Faline and a second fawn named Rusty are also mentioned.

Boot William Hage at Camp Waldron poses with Cleo and her new litter of puppies. Another report out of Camp Waldron stated that a deer broke into the swimming pool, swam around the tank, and then bounded out back into the woods.

Arthur A. Johnson of Camp Waldron poses with two of Farragut's cutest mascots, Sad Sack on the left and Skipper on the right. "They're a fine blend of spaniel and collie and should grow up to be real Navy dogs." The February 24, 1944, *Farragut News* also noted that both dogs had short hair "in true trainee fashion."

Five

SHIPS SERVICE

When Farragut was constructed, in addition to the training camps, the plans also called for low-cost housing for the Ships Service personnel. This became known as Farragut Village and was located just outside the main gate. Initially it contained 300 apartments, but it was expanded in 1944 to 500 in combinations of one, two, and three bedrooms. It also contained five dormitories with 43 rooms each.

The village was also a community that included all the basic necessities such as telephone facilities, a civilian dispensary with a 20-bed capacity, and a small complete laboratory, scullery, and clinic with a maximum capacity of 150. In addition, it had an auditorium with a seating capacity of 700, complete with motion picture booth and equipment, a barbershop and beauty parlor, a club, and library room.

FARRAGUT SCHOOL was rarely even seen by recruits, but this was an important phase of Farragut Village which housed some 2,000 civilian personnel and Ship's Company crewmen and their families. The school opened in April 1944 with an enrollment of 151 pupils. The Village, at No. 6 on the aerial photo, consisted of 99 buildings, with 500 apartments for married personnel and five dormitories for unmarried staffers. Apartments rented for $25 to $35 per month.

The needs of children were also included, such as an obstetrical department, nursery, a school with a capacity of 350 pupils that had an auditorium with a seating capacity of 250, a cafeteria with a seating capacity of 178, a playground measuring 250 feet by 500 feet that included a 40-foot wading pool along with a playpen and standard playground equipment, and a nursery with a capacity of 40 children.

"The Nerve Center of Farragut" proclaimed a *Farragut News* headline. In its day, the Central Administration Building was a modern, two-story building whose principle function was the operation of the Farragut Naval Training Station. It faced a field that became a parade ground and, as pictured above, was landscaped with flower beds and a green lawn.

Pictured are a few of the many Ships Service personnel who worked in the various administrative offices, keeping things shipshape and running smoothly. In October 1943, the *Farragut News* also announced that Farragut's Ships Service was "Idaho's biggest business."

Although women were not trained at the station, WAVES (Women Accepted for Voluntary Emergency Services) came on board in 1943 and took part in the daily operation of the facility to relieve sailors for overseas duty or other war efforts. The arrival of the first two WAVES, Anna M. Frombach, pharmacist mate third class, and Virginia M. Haglund, hospital apprentice, was announced in the June 19, 1943, edition of the *Farragut News*.

WAVES served as nurses, clerical staff, and provided transportation, along with other assignments. By October 27, 1944, there were 338 WAVES working at the station. Several sources recorded that eventually over 600 WAVES were employed there. The WAVES also had basketball, bowling, and softball teams, and were allowed to fire at the outdoor range if they qualified on an indoor range with a score of 140 or better. Pictured here is Deane Hintz, Y1c.

Mail call was no doubt the highlight of many a boot's day, with the much-anticipated letter from home or that someone special. During December 1942, the station post office handled 1,500,000 pieces of first class mail, plus 106,000 pieces of parcel post. By April 1943, that number had risen to 2,000,000 pieces and grew to over 3,000,000 by August, not counting parcel post and magazines.

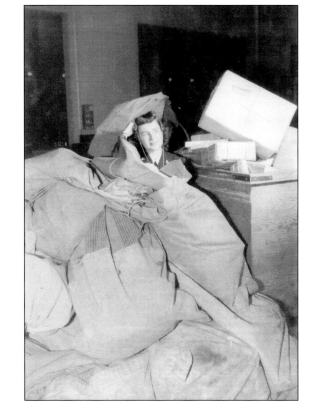

Each camp had a branch post office, as did the hospital. Mail was handed out twice a day. Here Joyce Fleming poses with the overwhelming amount of mail that the station processed. This photograph was taken in 1944.

"'I Want You For Christmas' was the title of a popular song enacted above by Camp Hill receptionist Juyne Thornton and recruit John Armstrong, Company 901, who is wrapped and tagged by the attractive Juyne 'ready for shipment' back home to the folks." This photograph and caption were published in the December 16, 1943, *Farragut News*.

Keeping the boots' uniforms fitted was no small task. Each was issued 15 pieces of clothing, which often required alterations, resulting in over 5,000 alterations per day. The tailor shop, managed by a civilian tailor, required 75 personnel (minimum) to operate it. They also performed uniform alterations for officers and chief petty officers as well as naval dependents' clothing. Locating enough staff was an ongoing problem.

By November 1943, the station's automatic telephone system handled over 24,000 calls daily. Hundreds of others, including long distance calls, were completed by a manually operated system. By August 1945, the station had 1,000 phones and 50 pay phones. Standing in the picture are Penny Mac Cabe of San Francisco, California, and Lt. H. D. Drumond, USNR, of Skellytown, Texas. Sitting from left to right are Georgia Southwell (supervisor) of San Diego, California, Mary Nelson of Hayden Lake, Idaho, and Bonnie Dobson, S1c., of Omaha, Nebraska.

SWITCHBOARD OPERATING was among the duties taken over by Waves when they began arriving at Farragut in June 1944. The first contingent consisted of only 29, but before Farragut was decommissioned there were about 600 Waves serving in numerous capacities throughout the base.

The cobbler shop solved the boots' shoe dilemma. They attached a neoprene half-sole over the leather sole, removed the heel, and inserted a lift between the shoe and the heel. When a boot graduated, the shoes were returned, the rubber half-soles and heel-lift were removed, and a new heel applied. The shop of 25, managed by a civilian, processed over 700 pairs of shoes daily, plus repairs for naval personnel and dependents. (Courtesy of ISHS, 1991-43.200.)

Although the boots did their own washing, when the laundry was put into service, it was considered to be the largest in the world. The laundry used over 2,500 pounds of soap a month. Over 225,000 pieces of laundry and dry cleaning were processed each week. A civilian manager oversaw 193 civilians and 32 enlisted men who worked two and sometimes three daily shifts to keep up with demand.

Ships Service stores and eating facilities employed hundreds of civilians recruited from the surrounding countryside. Civilian help or the lack thereof was a continuing problem due to the station's isolation. Wives of the Ships Service men were also employed, but they left when their husbands received orders to ship out. Pictured here are the Ships Service laundry workers at their second anniversary dinner on December 15, 1944.

Great Lakes and San Diego training stations experienced staffing problems even though they were located near metropolitan areas, but their difficulties were small compared to those encountered at Farragut. The isolation of the station was directly responsible for a large percentage of the manpower problems encountered by the entire center. Pictured are some of the Ships Service personnel at Camp Ward.

Compounding the manpower problem, construction work of all types was taken over by the navy on March 6, 1943, when the contractor's work terminated. This resulted in civil service employees hired by the navy and bluejackets completing the work, thus removing them from jobs they were recruited to perform. Work details taught boots that any kind of assignment could occur during their navy career. This photograph was taken c. May 8, 1943.

Procurement of fresh food was a continuing problem. Early in 1943, a new bakery was put into operation by the commissary department capable of producing 8,000 loaves of bread daily and 700 pies an hour. Milk was trucked in, obtained from dairies in many instances over 100 miles from the station. Huge warehouses and cold storage facilities made possible a constant flow of foodstuffs for the many mess halls.

Each mess hall measured 408 feet by 120 feet, with a 75-foot-by-80-foot kitchen annex. There were 92 ship's cooks assigned to each mess hall in addition to numerous mess cooks who peeled potatoes, served on the line handing out food, washed dishes, and performed other chores around the mess hall.

Fresh from civilian life and the problems related to food rationing, meals in the mess hall were quite the contrast. Using compartmented stainless steel trays took some getting used to, but they seemed a small price to pay for meals such as steak or chicken a la king. Desserts were apple-raisin pie, peach cobbler, or individually wrapped servings of ice cream. Most sailors agreed that they ate well at the station.

Each mess hall could feed 5,000 sailors in two shifts of 2,500 in an hour and a half. Here Tom Emery helps prepare a meal of fried pork chops, whipped potatoes, and country gravy. Prior to enlisting in the service, Emery was the broiler manager at Salt Lake City's Hotel Utah. This photograph is believed to have actually been taken in a recreation center's kitchen in 1945.

At the navy man's store, sailors could buy cigarettes (tax-free by the carton), stationery, extra things to eat (there were attached cafeterias), and keepsakes to send home to his girlfriend or family. "Stocking it up with cigarettes, food and candy for the long trip home are these members of Company 6031. All of the hundreds of 'boot' companies before them have been accorded the same privilege before going on recruit leave," according to a March 15, 1945, article in the *Farragut News*.

The sailors never forgot about their mothers, fathers, and sweethearts back home. Ship's stores went through tons of paper, pencils, envelopes, and postage each month. They also sold books, magazines, sweetheart pillows, jewelry, cigarettes, stuffed animals, sunglasses, personal care products, and a myriad of other personal and souvenir-related items. Pictured here is a sampling of the many items available in one of the Ships Service stores.

This Ships Service store on wheels served the outlying areas. Manned by Joseph V. Liuzzi, S2c., of Denver, Colorado, it made daily rounds to the brig area, fire department, Camp Scott rifle range, and the boat docks. The wheeled counter could be rolled onto any available truck. Marine Corps Pfc. E. T. Moore of Long Beach, California, buys some laundry supplies. Candy and soft drinks were also available during Sunday's ball games.

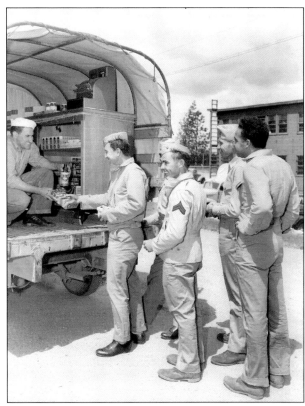

The *Farragut News*, distributed weekly, provided news about the station and the surrounding communities. The name was chosen from the 560 submitted. Six recruits received credit for the name and a $5 award. Those six were C. F. McDougall, Floyd Watts, E. G. Armstrong, Robert B. Holmes, Carlos R. Trujillo, and William R. Wright. Pictured here in March 1944 is Herbert Johnson, at age 18 from Des Moines, Iowa, of Camp Scott's Company 118.

Here Hugh Lago, Y3c(R), briefs an outgoing unit (OGU) work detail just before the truckload of *Farragut News* starts on its way from the loading dock. The edition these sailors are about to distribute announces the naming of Camp Gilmore, which opened on June 26, 1944. The first edition of the paper was published on December 12, 1942, and the final edition rolled out on June 13, 1946.

The hospital opened on January 17, 1943, and received its first patients on January 25. It was the largest and most modern hospital in the northwest, and contained all the modern equipment necessary for the practice of medicine and surgery. It was located near the end of the peninsula and had 7.5 miles of corridors. This photograph shows part of the hospital complex.

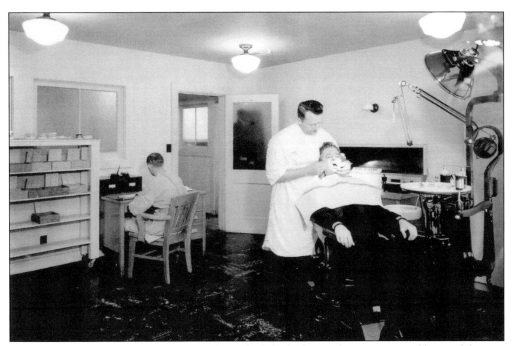

Over 11,000 surgical procedures were performed while the hospital was active, and hospital dentists provided for more than 58,500 individual sittings or visits. The laboratory performed more than 317,500 tests; the pharmacy compounded and dispensed nearly 88,000 prescriptions.

Pictured here is an aerial view of the hospital and Camp Bennion. The reported number of beds in the hospital varies depending on the source, but a report by Commodore Kelley dated August 14, 1945, stated that the hospital originally had 1,477 beds but was expanded in 1944 to an overload capacity of approximately 3,800 beds. This was made possible by the use of bunk beds.

In 1945, when Camp Bennion was transferred to the hospital, an additional 1,600 beds became available. The actual hospital census on September 1, 1945, was 3,542. The hospital cared for military dependents as well; more than 480 babies were born at the Farragut hospital. The hospital was staffed by 1,099 officers, nurses, and enlisted personnel.

The hospital, initially built to care for recruits, changed missions when in 1944 thousands of sailors and marines injured and wounded in the Pacific theater arrived in waves for treatment and rehabilitation. Being a patient in the hospital did have the occasional perk; you just might have lunch with a celebrity like Rita Hayworth. Seated on her left is Pfc. Peronna Angelo and on her right is Pvt. Joseph S. Stucki.

In addition to the main hospital, an outpatient ward was available to dependent families of naval personnel living on or near the station. The nativity scene pictured here in front of the hospital's administration building was life-sized and constructed in December 1943 by Al G. Renner, pharmacist mate first class, from Pasadena, California. It was illuminated at night and drew a lot of attention.

The practice of treating patients with only minor ills or injuries in the sick bays and dispensaries in the training camps was continued. The more serious and convalescent cases were transferred to the main hospital. Pictured here is a contingent of the hospital's WAVES undergoing an inspection.

In conjunction with the hospital, a school for training hospital corpsmen was established; it was operated, however, under a separate command from the main training station. It was reported that at Farragut there were more medical and dental officers on duty than there were in the entire U.S. Navy prior to Pearl Harbor. This photograph is of the staff at the hospital and is dated June 1, 1945.

The chaplains conducted religious services adapted to most Christian denominations. Their offices were located on the second deck of the Recreation Center. The *Service Schools Student Handbook* stated, "The Chaplain is your friend and confidant. He is not only the representative of the church, but is also a man you should talk to and know . . . he is capable of helping you in many ways . . . and [can] advise you on domestic relations, allotment of pay, wills, estates, education problems etc."

Reserve dental standards for draftees and enlistees were drastically lowered in 1943. Many recruits accepted for the reserve required partial or full plates and a variety of prosthetic work. This photograph was taken on December 21, 1944, and is of the dental prosthetic laboratory. Prior to the lowering of dental standards, routine dental work was accomplished in the recruit training camps.

The station's dental facility performed over 70,000 fillings in September 1943. Plans for a $500,000 dental laboratory staffed by 80 dental officers and 258 enlisted men, including 130 skilled dental technicians, were drawn up in late 1943. Pictured here is the inside of a dental X-ray room.

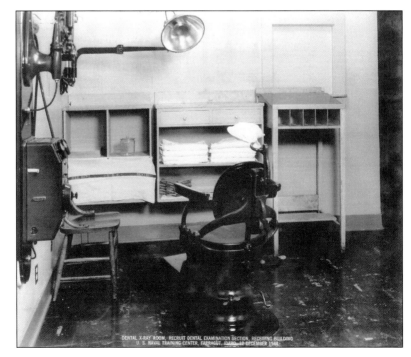

The dental laboratory building consisted of two decks, with laboratories and offices on the first deck and a dental technician school on the upper deck. When in operation, the new laboratory was geared to turn out 2,000 complete or partial plates a month. Pictured here is Capt. W. Rehraler, one of the many dentists who worked at the station.

Aside from the firefighting training the boots underwent, the station itself had four fire stations and one fireboat on the lake equipped with Chrysler high-pressure pumps. The station's fire stations consisted of seven modern firefighting units with the latest equipment. Pictured here is the fireboat with the pumps in action.

Posing with one of the station's fire trucks and a new litter of pups are Dave E. O'Bryan, S2c., from El Monte, California; Earl Thomas, S1c., from Waukon, Iowa; and Fabian Henrick, S1c., from Chicago, Illinois. The station also had 50 fully equipped fire watch lookout stations.

Jack E. Richards, S2c., the man in charge of working parties at the boat docks, is pictured here with "pole, line, pine, coffee pot and bait bucket," according to a May 15, 1943, *Farragut News* article. The Ships Service stores also sold fishing gear and rented out welfare department rowboats, of which there were 17 for 20¢ per hour or 50¢ for three hours. Fishing licenses were a mere $2.

The Harbor Master's House, pictured here, was built on top of a boathouse in what is now called Scenic Bay. It was used to monitor the boat traffic and signal the sailors in their whaleboats during training. The structure has three windows with drop-down panels below them, along with an irregular shaping to allow maximum viewing. This structure will soon be undergoing restoration at Farragut State Park.

Capt. Frank H. Kelley, the station's second commandant, was a 38-year navy veteran, a 1910 graduate of the Naval Academy, and a World War I veteran, having served with the Asiatic fleet. Prior to arriving at Farragut, he was in command of the USS *West Point*. Kelley succeeded I. C. Sowell in June 1943 and was promoted to commodore in September 1944. Kelley was married, with three service-member sons and two daughters.

The station also had a prison. Built of concrete blocks, the brig served as a confinement facility for unruly boots with barred windows and gates, jail cells, and support facilities. When a prisoner was escorted by armed marine guards, he was transported past 12-foot steel gates into the central courtyard. After processing, he was placed in a 4-or-6-man cell or solitary confinement to begin serving his sentence.

Pictured is mealtime for Bambi, the brig's resident deer. The firewood pictured here in the courtyard was hand cut by the prisoners, a form of hard labor punishment. The wood was used during the winter by the station's residential buildings for heat. For exercise, prisoners were forced to run the interior courtyard's perimeter 75 times each morning. The term *brig* is an abbreviation for brigantines, when navy prisons were ships at sea.

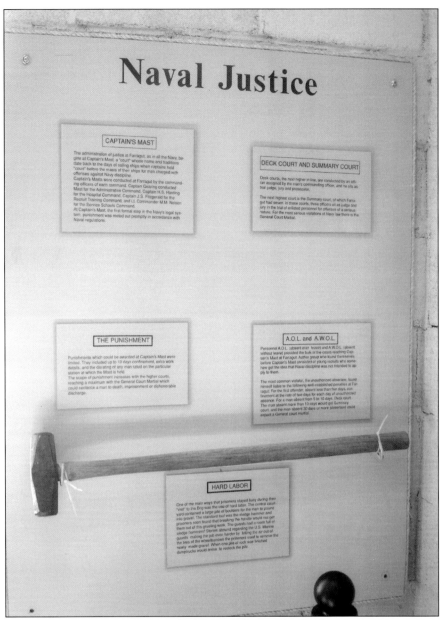

Naval Justice

CAPTAIN'S MAST

The administration of justice at Farragut, as in all the Navy, begins at Captain's Mast, a "court" whose name and traditions date back to the days of sailing ships when captains held "court" before the mast of their ships for men charged with offenses against Navy discipline.

Captain's Masts were conducted at Farragut by the commanding officers of each command. Captain Gearing conducted Mast for the Administrative Command, Captain H.S. Harting for the Hospital Command, Captain J.S. Fitzgerald for the Recruit Training Command, and Lt. Commander M.M. Nelson for the Service Schools Command.

At Captain's Mast, the first formal step in the Navy's legal system, punishment was meted out promptly in accordance with Naval regulations.

DECK COURT AND SUMMARY COURT

Deck courts, the next higher in line, are conducted by an officer assigned by the man's commanding officer, and he sits as trial judge, jury and prosecutor.

The next highest court is the Summary court, of which Farragut had seven. In these courts, three officers sit as judge and jury in the trial of enlisted personnel for offenses of a serious nature. For the most serious violations of Navy law there is the General Court Martial.

THE PUNISHMENT

Punishments which could be awarded at Captain's Mast were limited. They included up to 10 days confinement, extra work details, and the disrating of any man rated on the particular station at which the Mast is held.

The scope of punishment increases with the higher courts, reaching a maximum with the General Court Martial which could sentence a man to death, imprisonment or dishonorable discharge.

A.O.L. and A.W.O.L.

Personnel A.O.L. (absent over leave) and A.W.O.L. (absent without leave) provided the bulk of the cases reaching Captain's Mast at Farragut. Author group who found themselves before Captain's Mast consisted of young recruits who somehow got the idea that Naval discipline was not intended to apply to them.

The most common violator, the unauthorized absentee, found himself liable to the following well-established penalties at Farragut: For the first offender, absent less than five days, confinement at the rate of two days for each day of unauthorized absence. For a man absent from 5 to 10 days, Deck court. The man absent more than 10 days would get Summary court, and the man absent 30 days or more (desertion) could expect a General court martial.

HARD LABOR

One of the main ways that prisoners stayed busy during their "visit" to the Brig was the use of hard labor. The central court yard contained a large pile of boulders for the men to pound into gravel. The standard tool was the sledge hammer and prisoners soon found that breaking the handle would not get them out of this grueling work. The guards had a room full of sledge hammers! Stories abound regarding the U.S. Marine guards making the job even harder by letting the air out of the tires of the wheelbarrows the prisoners used to remove the newly made gravel. When one pile of rock was finished dumptrucks would arrive to restock the pile.

Unlike most of the station's buildings, the brig was designed to be fire resistant, as its occupants could not escape in the event of fire. The brig's normal capacity was 160 prisoners, with a maximum capacity of 240. It also had a wire mesh fence and watchtowers with floodlights. During the day, the prisoner performed hard labor using sledgehammers similar to the one pictured here to smash boulders into gravel. Those with severe offenses were placed in solitary confinement, a series of twelve 5-by-7.5-foot concrete cells and were fed bread and water—also known as "P and P" (piss and punk). They were then transported to the federal penitentiary at Treasure Island, California. Although being absent over leave or absent without leave made up the majority of offenses, Robert Sanders, Camp Waldron, 1943, confessed to spending three days in the brig's solitary section while at the station. His crime? Using the *F* word to a third class electrician mate. The charge was insubordination, and his subsistence consisted of bread and water.

Posing with Bambi at the brig are Armond G. Poirier, S2c., cook at the "Greystone Hotel;" Ensign Mathew H. Whitman of the public relations department; and Arthur P. Oretega, S2c., and John B. Fisher, S2c., both brig guards. Rip the police dog is unsure what to make of the situation. This photograph ran in the September 18, 1943, *Farragut News* and was captioned, "Brig holds no fear for this fawn deer."

Frankie Meilke, the cashier, was the only known woman to be confined to the brig. While crossing the grinder to tell her husband that their baby had died, she was arrested and placed in the brig. Fortunately a chaplain was able to intervene and coordinate her release. Regrettably the three brothers pictured here were killed when their ship was bombed.

USS INTREPID   USN PHOTO

Ships in commission increased from 913 on January 1, 1942, to 4,167 on January 1, 1944. To keep up with this increased need for personnel, training periods were shortened. All departments cut rosters and assumed more work so that more personnel could be transferred to sea duty. Ray A. Raine, S1c. (GM), attended gunner's mate training at the station, graduating on May 13, 1944. He was later assigned to the USS *Intrepid*.

At least one member of the Ships Service went on to earn a place in history. Don W. Samuelson, employed as a weapons instructor and gunsmith, went on to become a state senator and then governor of Idaho, serving from January 2, 1967, to January 4, 1971. This photograph, believed to have been taken after his term as governor, is of Samuelson fishing on Lake Pend Oreille. (Courtesy of ISHS, 72-190.241c.)

Six

NEW MISSIONS

Two years and two months after the first recruit training camp was commissioned, the Bureau of Personnel announced that Farragut would discontinue taking recruits, and the training station would be decommissioned. By the time this decision was made, nearly 300,000 men had been trained at Farragut.

As the inflow of new recruits stopped, all departments on the station were able to make more and more personnel available for transfer; it was a gradual and planned process. All service schools were scheduled to close May 1, 1945. This photograph is believed to be of Gerald Weed, Marven Weed, Lonnie Weed, and Everett Dale Weed, of Orient, Iowa.

During the closing months of the war, Farragut had a Separation Center where personnel were sent for discharge. Although the station was not a high-volume separation point, in 1945, it processed just over 600 men, and in 1946, roughly 4,025 officers and men made their way home through the station's efforts.

HAPPY DAYS! During the closing months of the war, Farragut had a "Separation Center" where personnel were sent for discharge. Here's a group lined up for the happy occasion which saw them pick up their discharge papers, severance pay, and travel funds to take them back home to their loved ones. Note "Hash marks" and service ribbons proudly worn by several of these veterans.

On June 1, 1945, a Personal Effects Distribution Center was established in Camp Hill. Staffed by roughly 70 personnel, their mission was to receive from overseas the effects of men killed in the war, inventory them for objectionable or censorable matter and government-issued equipment, launder the clothing, polish the buttons and jewelry, and put the items in storage until the next of kin's wishes were received regarding disposition.

More than 200 German prisoners of war arrived at the station in February 1945 and were interred at the Butler Overflow area, the area where Butler Construction had their administrative offices. These were Germans captured by U.S. troops in Europe and Africa, and as there were no neutral countries in Europe in which to confine them, they were brought to the United States.

The prisoners were escorted by army troops, and they were guarded by an army unit comprised of roughly 75 officers and men while confined on the station. The prisoner population began with 750 but eventually increased to 850. One report places the number at 926. The prisoners were used to clear brush, perform maintenance work, shovel coal, and perform any labor jobs that needed doing.

A memo issued on February 8, 1945, by Capt. Hilyer F. Gearing, the assistant commander of the station, stated, "The prisoner of war is a soldier, not a criminal . . . he is entitled to respect. He is not to be subjected to insult, may not be abused or sworn at . . . It is the duty of Heads of Departments using prisoner of war labor to instruct subordinate personnel to comply with these instructions."

The POWs filled a vital role working as groundskeepers, bakers, storekeepers, cooks, laborers, and forest firefighters. Many felt they had it better than the boots and were hesitant to write home, for fear their treatment would change. Idaho had at least 10 POW camps; some sources record 22. These camps provided local farmers the workers to harvest their crops, such as potatoes, beets, and lettuce. Idaho had two POW base camps, one at Farragut and the other in Rupert. (Courtesy of ISHS, 77-103.11a.)

Meals prepared by the POWs at Farragut became very popular with the station's officers looking for a break from the regular meals of SOS. Here the POWs sort through boxes of canned goods. The POW camp was inactivated on April 25, 1946.

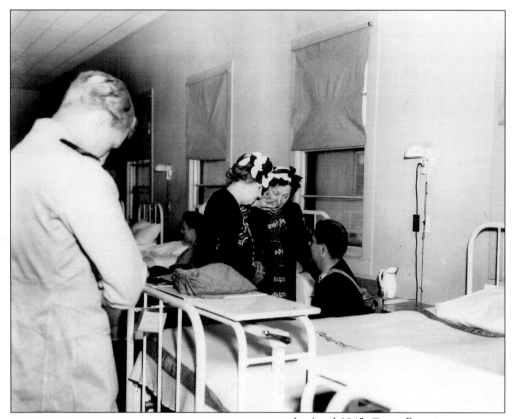

In April 1945, Camp Bennion was closed for basic training and took on a new mission. Due to the large numbers of men wounded in the Pacific theater, it became the overflow area for the hospital. In addition, 1,600 more beds were made available for treating neuropsychiatric patients, those who were mentally, not physically, ill. This photograph is believed to be Helen Keller, on the left, visiting hospital patients c. 1946.

On April 12, 1945, America and its allies were stunned when Pres. Franklin D. Roosevelt passed away. The station, the nation, and the world mourned his passing. Pictured here, the flag in front of the Central Administration Building was lowered to half-staff in tribute, and it flew in this position for 30 days.

Seven

END OF AN ERA
AND NEW BEGINNINGS

In the late 1940s, Idaho's Department of Fish and Game bought parcels of land along the shoreline, leading to a larger agreement wherein most of the remaining land was given to the state as the Farragut Wildlife Management Area. Efforts were made to form flocks of pheasants to help with game propagation. The pheasants refused to cooperate and would not hatch their eggs. Bantam hens were brought in to remedy the situation.

"End of the Trail"

Farragut Naval Center
DECOMMISSIONED
JUNE 15, 1946

C. W. Neida (center) plants a flower bed for the front of a recreation building with his two right-hand men. On the left is Arnold W. Klug, who was associated with the Idaho Forestry Service, and on the right is Homer P. Golding, formerly of Idaho Soil Conservation Service. This photograph was taken sometime in 1945.

On Saturday, June 15, 1946, in a gray mist and drizzling rain, the Farragut Naval Training Station was decommissioned. Perhaps the feelings of those present were best expressed by the commandant: "It is a gloomy day to wind up a gloomy business."

In the spring of 1946, when the station's pending closure became known, the VFW, various chambers of commerce, civic leaders, and individuals who represented institutions of higher learning contacted senators from Idaho, Washington, Oregon, and Montana regarding turning the station into a nonprofit college. The idea was well received, and the Farragut College and Technical Institute opened in October with 23 faculty members and Admiral Kelley, former commander, as president of the board of directors. The institute occupied most of the buildings on the peninsula, and the student union building was a former officers club. The focus was primarily on the returning veterans and interest grew. By January 2, 1947, the facility had 56 faculty members and a combined total of 1,000 students in the technical institute and college division. A short period of time later, interest in the institution began to wane as veterans transitioned to the civilian world. On or about May 1949, the facility closed due to lack of funds and low enrollment. Pictured here is a 1947 Christmas photograph of the college chorus.

After the station fell into disuse, most of the buildings were either torn down or dismantled and recycled. Some, however, were saved and relocated to surrounding communities. Here a building from the hospital complex begins its journey to the Bonner hospital where it will become part of that complex. A number of buildings are known to have gone to Washington State University at Pullman.

Pictured here in a December 1950 photograph is the former Blackwell Mansion and residence of Commodore Kelley, the station's commander. From 1952 to 1965, this house also served as the Fish and Game Headquarters at the Farragut Wildlife Management Area. Buster Owsley of Hagerman, Idaho, a Department of Fish and Game employee, poses in front of the former mansion. By 1951, most of the buildings on the former station had been razed.

A 20-acre parcel of the former station was retained for an acoustic research detachment for the U.S. Navy, which is still in operation today. The facility is involved in research and development designed to make ships and submarines operate more quietly. It employs roughly 100 employees and contractors. Its programs support navy systems commands and other defense agencies, as well as private industry and research efforts of the United Kingdom. (Photograph by Steve O'Neal.)

In the 1960s, scouting organizations looking for areas with infrastructure suitable for large encampments found the former station and developed part of it for jamborees. This photograph was taken during the 1967 World Jamboree. This public use resulted in approximately two-thirds of the land being returned to the federal government, and reissued in 1965 to the newly formed Idaho Department of Parks and Recreation, creating a cooperative management as Farragut State Park.

In 1982, part of the Idaho National Guard held its annual summer camp at the park and helped with the renovation at the Locust Grove shelter, an area formally part of the hospital complex. They also helped fill in the former sewage treatment area, which is pictured here. According to a plaque at the park, the work was performed by "2nd Platoon, Co B 116E ID NG, Orofino Id."

The Idaho Army National Guard also found the former station's infrastructure suitable to its needs, as is evidenced by the this bivouac photograph of their 1982 encampment.

Eight

GONE BUT NOT FORGOTTEN

Today the majority of the area that made up the station is now Farragut State Park. This sign gives today's visitors to the park a brief overview of the park's history and is located right next to the park visitor's center. Of the 776 buildings that comprised the station, very few remain today.

The brig is one of the few remaining structures that comprised the station. It has been transformed into a small museum by Idaho's Department of Parks and Recreation and contains memorabilia dedicated to those who worked and trained at Farragut. In 2002, the brig was added to the National Register of Historic Places. Pictured above is a recently restored vintage 1938 Ford truck, parked in the brig's compound.

Some of the cells in the brig are in their original configuration; others have been converted to house interpretive displays, an audiovisual theater, and a gift shop. Pictured here are Farragut veterans and their families touring the museum at the 2008 annual reunion. The three flags on the wall to the viewer's right were actual company flags, and are those pictured in the company graduation photographs.

Each year, the first weekend after Labor Day, Farragut veterans and their families return to the former station for an annual reunion. Some can still wear their uniforms, and all proudly relate their stories to those wanting to learn more about the station or their actions during World War II. Here two members of the greatest generation salute the colors during the flag raising ceremony at the 2008 reunion.

This vintage 1942 Farragut Naval Training Station Pirsch fire truck is also parked in the brig courtyard. The fire truck was painstakingly restored and unveiled to the public on September 9, 2006, at the annual Farragut veterans' reunion.

Pictured here is a remnant of Camp Bennion's Ready Magazine, used to store live ammunition for the camp's indoor rifle range. All of the camps except Gilmore had a magazine; most are still standing. Although long since repainted, some still bear faint red lettering of the cautionary. A look inside may reveal names of veterans who trained there. The plaque gives a brief history of the camp's namesake, Captain Bennion.

After the camp was decommissioned, there was discussion on what to do with the area that had comprised the sewage treatment plant. An architect was consulted, and it was converted to a picnic area, which is known today as the Sunrise Day Use Area. This is also the location of the annual Farragut veterans' reunion. Pictured here is part of the Sunrise Day Use Area and Lake Pend Oreille.

Visitors to today's Farragut State Park can drive on the original roads and view two of the remaining landmarks, the water towers, which are still in use today. This vintage water tower is located in the area where the hospital complex once stood.

Mack, a large bronze bust of a U.S. sailor, is located in the Farragut Memorial Plaza, next to the Brig Museum. It represents the 293,381 sailors who trained at the station. This picture shows the path leading to the plaza, with *Mack* visible in the background behind the flagpole.

Mack's face has the serious gaze of the sailor serving his country with pride and is made up of many smaller faces (like the relief image on a coin) of those recruits who made him. Some of the faces are handsome and bold; some are awkward and endearing. They portray the naiveté and optimism of the young men who trained at the station.

Mack is positioned on a base that is reminiscent of a whaleboat—the rowboats the boots spent countless hours training in while learning the art of rowing in unison and the advantages of teamwork. Surrounding Mack and the whaleboat and facing the flagpole are 29 sets of footprints. Each is at attention and commemorates the number (in tens of thousands) of men who trained at the station.

Pictured here is a close up of one of the 29 sets of footprints, representing the 293,381 boots who trained at the Farragut Naval Training Station.

Today the former camps are campgrounds where park visitors can step back in time with a visit to the brig or enjoy all the scenery, fishing, hiking, and other outdoor activities that Idaho has to offer. Campers can bring their own RVs and tents, or if they chose, the park has cabins they can rent. Pictured here are two such cabins.

DISCOVER THOUSANDS OF LOCAL HISTORY BOOKS
FEATURING MILLIONS OF VINTAGE IMAGES

Arcadia Publishing, the leading local history publisher in the United States, is committed to making history accessible and meaningful through publishing books that celebrate and preserve the heritage of America's people and places.

Find more books like this at
www.arcadiapublishing.com

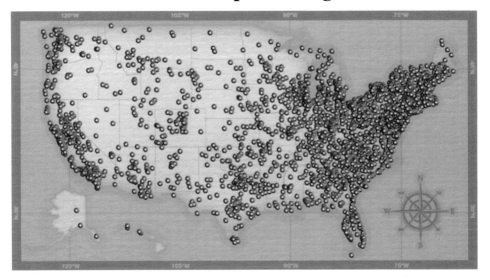

Search for your hometown history, your old
stomping grounds, and even your favorite sports team.

Consistent with our mission to preserve history on a local level, this book was printed in South Carolina on American-made paper and manufactured entirely in the United States. Products carrying the accredited Forest Stewardship Council (FSC) label are printed on 100 percent FSC-certified paper.

MADE IN THE